AF365134

ISBN : 9781655938825

SUMMARY

German Dance

German Dance N°7

Ludwig van Beethoven
Arrt.: Colette Mourey

2
Trio
p
1/2CIX
rit.
D.C. al Fine

For Elise

For Elise

Ludwig van Beethoven
Arrt.: Colette Mourey

15
pp
18
21
1.
2.
24
1/2CV
27
30
dim.

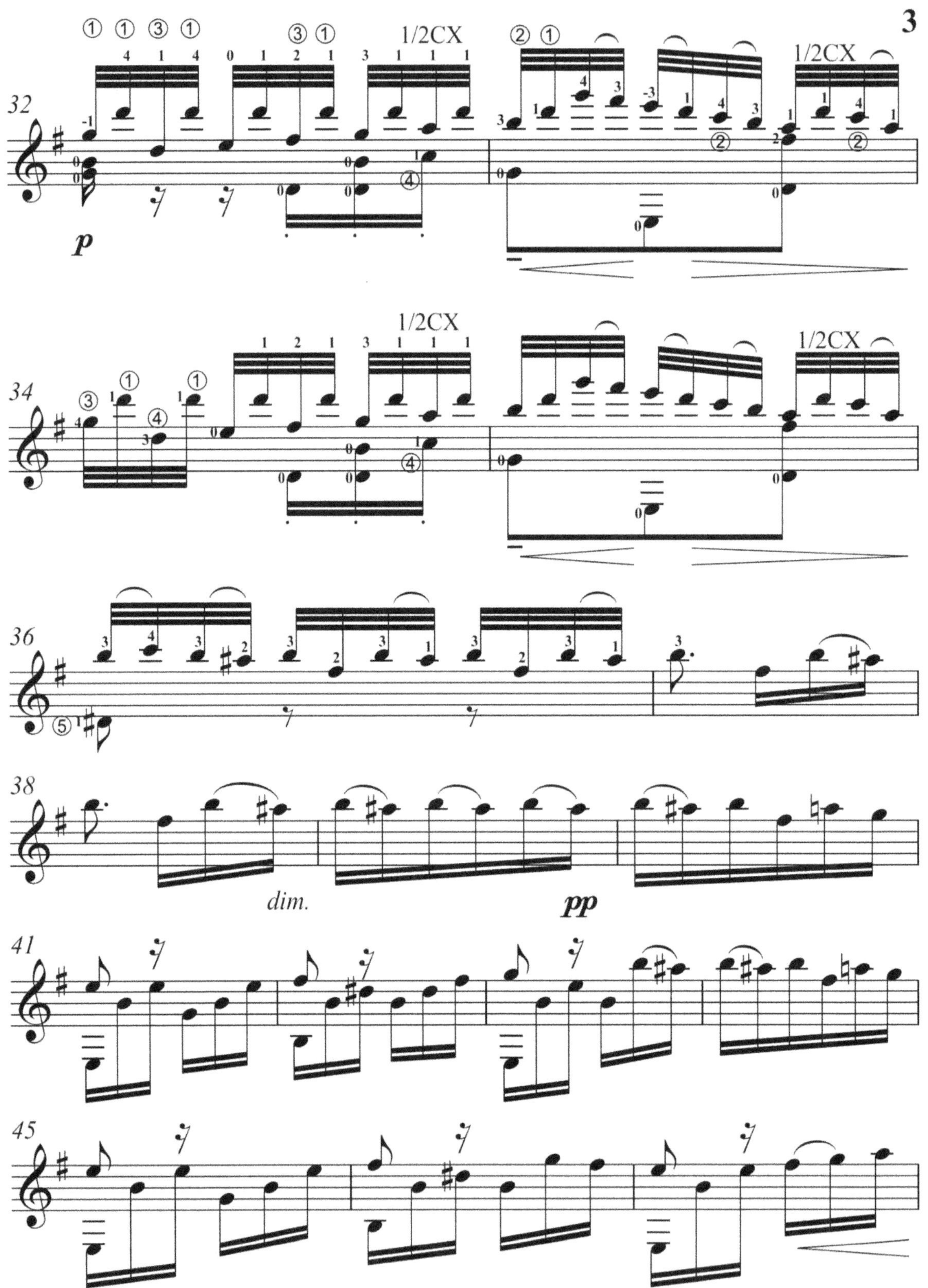
3
32
p
1/2CX
1/2CX
34
1/2CX
1/2CX
36
38
dim.
pp
41
45

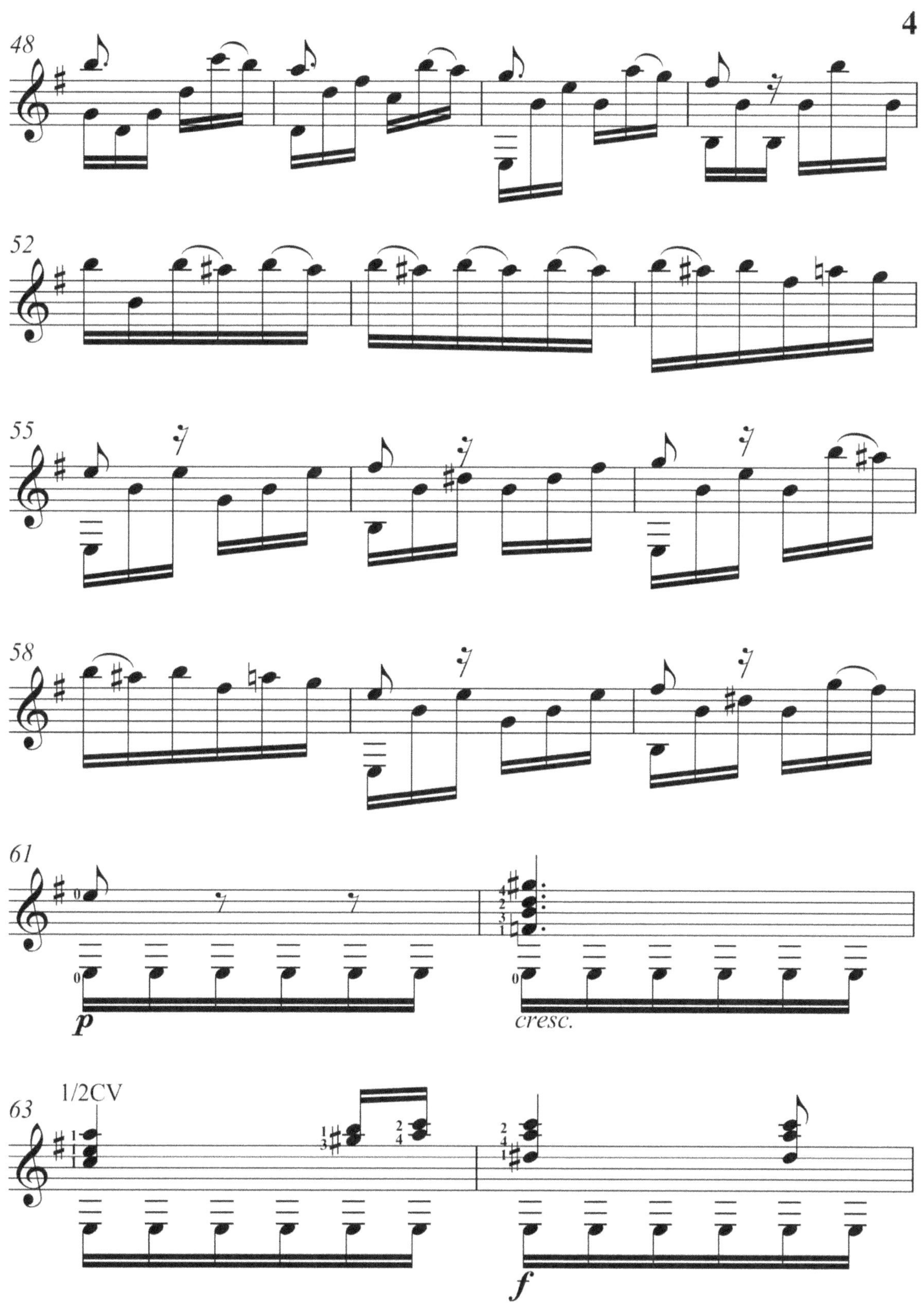

4
48
52
55
58
61
p
cresc.
63
1/2CV
f

5
65
dim.
67
CII
69
cresc.
1/2CV
71
CVIII
CIII
73
dim.
CI
CII
75
p

CII
78
pp
80
poco cresc.
82
dim.
84
pp
86
89
6

92
mf
95
dim.
98
101
Morendo
104

Ode to Joy

Ode to Joy
From 9th Symphony

Ludwig van Beethoven
Arrt.: Colette Mourey

Allegro assai ♩ = 80

Sonatina

Sonatina

Ludwig van Beethoven
Arrt.: Colette Mourey

1

2
18
21
24
27
1/2CV
mf
29
2
1/2CV
32
rit.

2.Romanze

Molto cantabile

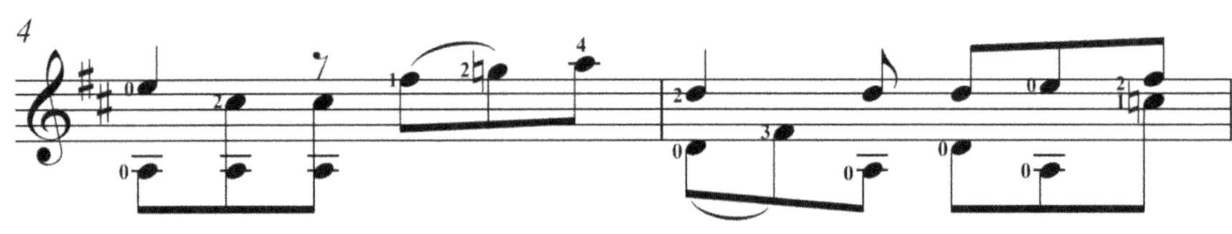

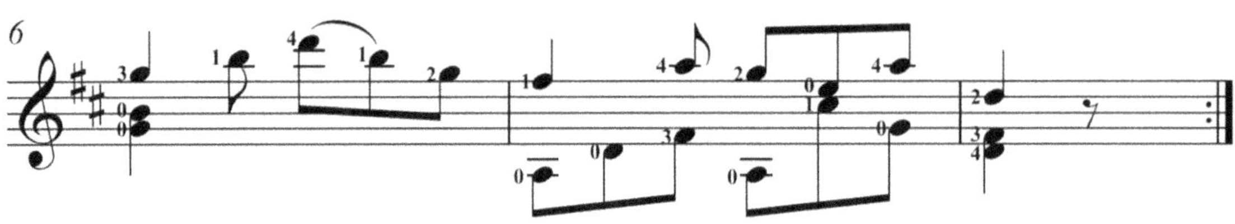

4

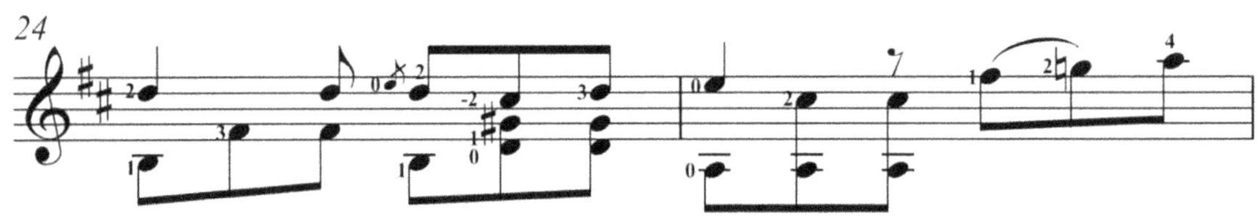

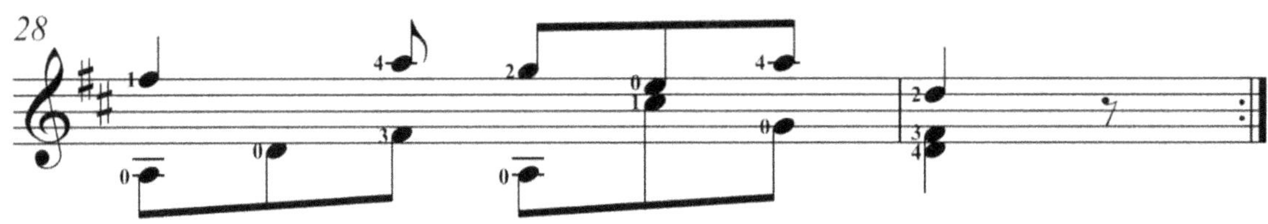

6
p
32
34
36
38
rit.

Waltz

Waltz

Ludwig van Beethoven
Arrt.: Colette Mourey

Moonlight Sonata

Moonlight Sonata op.27 N°2
First Movement
For Solo Guitar

Ludwig van Beethoven
Arrt.: Colette Mourey

Adagio sostenuto

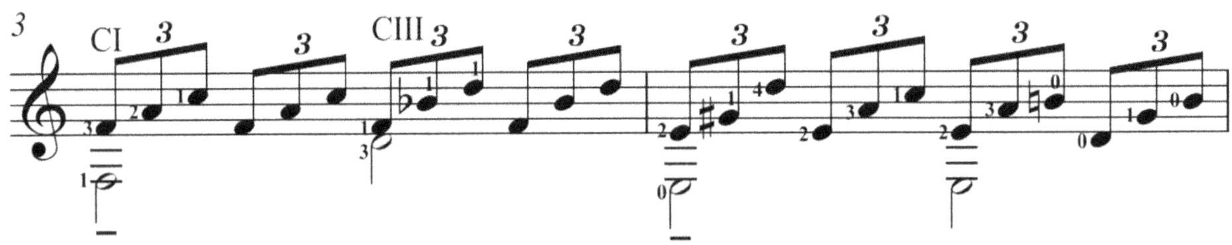

2
9
p i m
②
③
11
②
④ ③
⑥ ③
⑤
CIV
CI
③ ③
③
13
15
CIII
③ ②
③
②
③ ②
⑥
⑤
17
CIII
③ ②
③
②
③ ②
⑤
⑤
19
CIII
②

4
33
CII
1/2CV
35
37
39
dim.
41
43

5
cresc.
p
p i m
1/2CV
1/2CVI

6
57
cresc.
59
CII
p
pp
61
1/2CV
1/2CV
63
1/2CV
65
1/2CV
dim.
67
rit.
CV
pp

38

Minuet

Minuet

Ludwig van Beethoven
Arrt.: Colette Mourey

2
1/2CVII
1/2CVII
sfz
1/2CII
sfz
f
sfz
CII
sfz
sfz
p
1/2CVII
1/2CVII
sfz
f
1/2CII
sfz
sfz
CII
sfz
sfz

Trio
p
1/2CII
1/2CII

4
1/2CI
1/2CII
1.
2.
p
42
44
46
48

Beethoven for Guitar

TABLE DES MATIERES

47

ISBN : 9781655938825